Summer BBQ Fiesta

Cookbook

Flavorful Barbecue Recipes for Summer Partaay

By: Owen Davis

Copyright Notice!

Table of Contents

Introduction

There's more to barbecuing than placing a chunk of briskets on the wild flame of fire. That doesn't sound healthy in any way, for the record. To get the best sets of barbecue meals for your guests this summer, you'd have to get intentional with your recipe. Between marinating the steak the right way and roasting it under the right temperature to get that golden brown look - there are many details people miss out on when making barbecue.

In the next few recipes, we'd be explicit with the details. We advise that you stick to the measurements as you make your barbecue this summer. As you perfect each recipe, you could go ahead to tweak the ingredients to better suit your taste. With these recipes from the Summer BBQ Fiesta cookbook, your summer party is about to get juicier. Are you ready to get barbecuing? Let's get started!

1. Classic BBQ Baby Ribs

Get ready for a mouthwatering adventure as we dive into the world of Classic BBQ Ribs. I love these tender and succulent ribs. They are coated in a smoky, tangy barbecue sauce that will have your taste buds dancing with delight. Get your grill fired up and prepare for a flavor explosion that will make your summer barbecue unforgettable!

Serving Size: 4 servings

Marinating Time: 4 hours to overnight

Cooking Time: 2 hours

Ingredients

- 2 racks of pork baby back ribs (about 4-5 pounds total)
- 1/4 cup brown sugar
- 1 teaspoon black pepper
- 1 tablespoon salt
- 1 tablespoon onion powder
- 1 tablespoon garlic powder
- 1 tablespoon chili powder
- 2 tablespoons paprika
- 1/2 teaspoon cayenne pepper (optional, for added heat)
- 2 cups barbecue sauce

Instructions

Preparing the Dry Rub:

1- In a small-sized bowl, combine the paprika, brown sugar, onion powder, garlic powder, salt, black pepper, chili powder, and cayenne pepper (if using). Mix well to create the dry rub.

2- Sprinkle the dry rub evenly over both sides of the ribs, pressing it into the meat to adhere.

Grill the Ribs:

1- Place the ribs on the grill over indirect heat, bone side down.

2- Close the lid and let them cook for 1.5 to 2 hours, or until the meat is tender and starts to pull away from the bones.

3- Close the lid and let the sauce caramelize for a few minutes.

4- Remove the ribs from the grill and let them rest for about 10 minutes to allow the juices to redistribute.

2. Grilled Chicken Skewers BBQ

Let me Indulge you in the irresistible flavors of these Grilled Chicken Skewers BBQ. I delight in this smoky, juicy chicken because it will transport your taste buds to barbecue heaven. Tender chunks of marinated chicken are threaded onto skewers and grilled to perfection, creating a tantalizing smoky flavor that will have everyone coming back for seconds. Enjoy sharing this delicious meal with your loved ones and make lasting memories together!

Serving Size: 6 People

Marinating Time: 1 to 4 hours

Cooking Time: 10 to 15 minutes

Ingredients:

- 5 pounds boneless, skinless chicken breasts, cut into 1-inch cubes
- 1/4 cup olive oil
- 3 tablespoons soy sauce
- 3 tablespoons honey
- 2 tablespoons lemon juice
- 2 cloves garlic, minced
- 1 teaspoon paprika
- 1/2 teaspoon cumin
- 1/2 teaspoon black pepper
- 1/2 teaspoon salt
- Wooden skewers, soaked in water for 30 minutes

Instructions:

1- Marinate the chicken by combining olive oil, soy sauce, honey, lemon juice, minced garlic, paprika, cumin, black pepper, and salt.

2- Coat the chicken cubes with the marinade and refrigerate for 1 to 4 hours.

3- Grill the skewers on a preheated grill for 5 to 7 minutes per side until the chicken is cooked through and has a charred exterior.

4- Let the skewers rest before serving.

3. BBQ Pulled Pork Sandwiches

Prepare to experience a flavor-packed delight with these mouthwatering Pulled Pork Sandwiches. Tender and juicy pulled pork slow-cooked to perfection, is smothered in a tangy and sweet barbecue sauce, creating a sandwich that will leave you craving more. Mostly I enjoy this with loved ones as we get ready to savor the ultimate comfort food that makes our taste buds sing!

Serving Size: 12 servings

Cooking Time: 8 to 10 hours (slow cooker) or 6 to 8 hours (oven)

Ingredients:

- 4 pounds of pork shoulder or pork butt
- 1 tablespoon brown sugar
- 1 tablespoon paprika
- 1 tablespoon garlic powder
- 1 tablespoon onion powder
- 1 tablespoon salt
- 1 teaspoon black pepper
- 1 teaspoon cayenne pepper (optional, for added heat)
- 1 cup barbecue sauce
- 1/4 cup apple cider vinegar
- 1/4 cup chicken broth
- Hamburger buns or sandwich rolls
- Coleslaw (optional, for serving)

Instructions:

1- Prepare the pork by combining brown sugar, paprika, garlic powder, onion powder, salt, black pepper, and cayenne pepper to create a dry rub.

2- Coat the pork shoulder with a dry rub and let it sit for 15 minutes.

3- For the slow cooker method, place the seasoned pork shoulder in a slow cooker and pour a mixture of barbecue sauce, apple cider vinegar, and chicken broth over it. Cook on low heat for 8 to 10 hours.

4- For the oven method, preheat the oven to 325°F (163°C), place the seasoned pork shoulder in a roasting pan or Dutch oven, and pour the sauce mixture over it. Cook for 6 to 8 hours.

5- Once the pork is cooked, shred it using two forks and mix it with the cooking liquid.

6- Toast the buns and spoon the pulled pork onto the bottom half.

7- Add barbecue sauce and coleslaw if desired. Cover with the top bun.

8- Enjoy the Pulled Pork Sandwich.

4. Grilled Corn on the Cob

Embrace the sizzle of the grill and indulge in the delightful flavors of Grilled Corn on the Cob. Since I found this recipe, I enjoy this simple yet sensational dish at outdoor gatherings and create lasting memories with family and friends. Now you also can Enjoy the taste of summer at its finest!

Serving Size: 6 servings

Cooking Time: 10 to 15 minutes

Ingredients:

- Fresh corn on the cob, husks intact
- Butter
- Salt and pepper to taste
- Optional toppings: grated Parmesan cheese, chopped fresh herbs (such as cilantro or parsley), lime wedges

Instructions:

1- Gently peel back the husks, keeping them attached at the base.

2- Remove the silk strands and discard.

3- Carefully pull the husks back up to cover the corn.

4- Soak the corn in cold water for 10 minutes.

5- Place the soaked corn on the grill over direct heat.

6- Cook for 10 to 15 minutes, turning occasionally.

7- Spread softened butter generously over the corn.

8- Season with salt and pepper to taste.

9- Optionally, try toppings like grated Parmesan cheese, fresh herbs, or lime juice.

10- Arrange on a platter and serve immediately while warm.

5. BBQ Beef Brisket

The thoughts of this recipe alone make me salivate. Prepare to embark on a journey of smoky, melt-in-your-mouth goodness with this BBQ Beef Brisket recipe. The rich and flavorful beef is slow-cooked to perfection, resulting in tender slices that are infused with a tantalizing blend of spices and smoky barbecue sauce. Get ready to impress your guests and experience the ultimate BBQ delight that will have everyone coming back for seconds!

Serving Size: 2 servings

Marinating Time: 12 to 24 hours

Cooking Time: 8 to 10 hours

Ingredients:

- 5 to 6 pounds of beef brisket, trimmed of excess fat
- 1/4 cup brown sugar
- 1 tablespoon garlic powder
- 2 tablespoons paprika
- 2 tablespoons chili powder
- 1 tablespoon onion powder
- 1 tablespoon salt
- 1 teaspoon black pepper
- 1/2 teaspoon cayenne pepper (optional, for added heat)
- 2 cups barbecue sauce

Instructions:

1- Mix brown sugar, garlic powder, paprika, onion powder, chili powder, salt, black pepper, and cayenne pepper in a small bowl.

2- Mix well to create a dry rub.

3- Rub the dry rub all over the brisket, ensuring even coverage.

4- Place the seasoned brisket in a resealable bag or dish.

5- Pour barbecue sauce over the brisket, coating it thoroughly.

6- Seal the bag or cover the dish and refrigerate for 12 to 24 hours.

7- Cook the marinated brisket on the grill or in the oven.

8- Close the lid or cover it with foil to trap smoke and moisture.

9- Slow-cook for 8 to 10 hours until internal temperature reaches 195°F to 205°F (90°C to 96°C).

10- Remove the brisket from the grill or oven once it reaches the desired temperature.

6. Grilled Shrimp Skewers

One of my personal favorites for dessert. Elevate your grilling game with these succulent Grilled Shrimp Skewers. Bursting with flavor and cooked to perfection, these skewers are a seafood lover's delight. Whether you're hosting a backyard barbecue or simply craving a delicious and healthy meal, these grilled shrimp skewers will transport your taste buds to a tropical paradise and leave you wanting more!

Serving Size: 5 servings

Marinating Time: 30 minutes

Cooking Time: 5 to 7 minutes

Ingredients:

- 1 pound large shrimp, peeled and deveined
- 2 tablespoons olive oil
- 1 teaspoon paprika
- 1/2 teaspoon cumin
- 2 tablespoons lemon juice
- 2 cloves garlic, minced
- 1/2 teaspoon chili powder
- 1/2 teaspoon salt
- Wooden skewers, soaked in water for 30 minutes

Instructions:

1- In a bowl, combine olive oil, lemon juice, minced garlic, paprika, cumin, chili powder, salt, and black pepper.

2- Whisk to blend.

3- Marinate the shrimp in the mixture for 30 minutes.

4- Remove shrimp from the marinade, saving it for basting.

5- Skewer the marinated shrimp.

6- Grill for 2 to 3 minutes per side until pink and opaque.

7. BBQ Chicken Wings

Personally, this is my go-to BBQ to satisfy cravings. Delight your taste buds with these finger-licking BBQ Chicken Wings. Crispy on the outside and tender on the inside, these wings are coated in a smoky and tangy barbecue sauce that will have you coming back for more. Whether you're hosting a game night or simply craving a delicious appetizer, these BBQ chicken wings will take your taste buds on a flavor-packed adventure!

Serving Size: 8 People

Cooking Time: 35 to 40 minutes

Ingredients:

- 2 pounds chicken wings, tips removed and wings separated at the joint
- 1 cup barbecue sauce
- 2 tablespoons honey
- 2 tablespoons soy sauce
- 1 tablespoon Worcestershire sauce
- 1 teaspoon garlic powder
- 1 teaspoon paprika
- 1/2 teaspoon salt
- 1/4 teaspoon black pepper

Instructions:

1- Combine barbecue sauce, honey, soy sauce, Worcestershire sauce, garlic powder, paprika, salt, and black pepper in a bowl.

2- Mix well to make the marinade.

3- Add chicken wings to the bowl and coat them evenly.

4- Refrigerate for 1-2 hours to meld flavors.

5- Remove wings from the marinade, allowing excess to drip off.

6- Grill wings for 15-20 minutes, turning occasionally, until fully cooked with a crispy exterior.

7- Ensure internal temperature reaches 165°F (74°C).

8- Halfway through grilling, start basting wings with more barbecue sauce.

9- Generously brush sauce onto the wings.

10- Continue grilling and basting for 10-15 minutes until the sauce caramelizes and forms a sticky coating.

8. Grilled Vegetable Skewers Kabobs

Experience the vibrant flavors of summer with these Grilled Vegetable Kabobs. Bursting with colors and textures, these kabobs feature a medley of fresh vegetables, perfectly charred on the grill. The smoky aroma and delightful combination of flavors will take your outdoor gatherings to the next level. I enjoy serving this healthy and delicious option for vegetarians and veggie lovers alike.

Serving Size: 2 people

Marinating Time: 30 minutes (optional)

Cooking Time: 10 to 15 minutes

Ingredients:

- 1 red bell pepper, seeded and cut into chunks
- 1 yellow bell pepper, seeded and cut into chunks
- 1 green bell pepper, seeded and cut into chunks
- 1 red onion, cut into chunks
- 1 zucchini, sliced into rounds
- 1 yellow squash, sliced into rounds
- 8 to 10 cherry tomatoes
- 8 to 10 button mushrooms
- 3 tablespoons olive oil
- 2 tablespoons balsamic vinegar
- 2 cloves garlic, minced
- 1 teaspoon dried Italian seasoning
- 1/2 teaspoon salt
- 1/4 teaspoon black pepper
- Wooden skewers, soaked in water for 30 minutes

Instructions:

1- In a bowl, combine olive oil, balsamic vinegar, garlic, Italian seasoning, salt, and pepper.

2- Whisk until well blended.

3- Add vegetables to the bowl and gently toss to coat evenly.

4- Let them marinate for 30 minutes.

5- Remove vegetables from the marinade, saving any excess for basting.

6- Skewer vegetables, alternating types.

7- Place skewers on a preheated grill.

8- Grill for 10 to 15 minutes, turning occasionally, until tender and slightly charred.

9- Baste kabobs with reserved marinade while grilling.

10- Remove from the grill when cooked to perfection.

9. Smoked Pulled Chicken Sliders

With its tenderness, I always crave more of this. I Prepare this flavor-packed delight with these Smoked Pulled Chicken Sliders. Tender, smoky chicken is slow-cooked to perfection and then shredded, creating succulent bites that are enhanced with a tangy and savory barbecue sauce. These sliders are perfect for any gathering or game day event, offering a handheld treat that will have everyone reaching for seconds!

Serving Size: 4 Servings

Cooking Time: 3 to 4 hours

Ingredients:

- 4 boneless, skinless chicken breasts
- 1 tablespoon olive oil
- 1 teaspoon paprika
- 1 teaspoon garlic powder
- 1 teaspoon onion powder
- 1 teaspoon salt
- 1/2 teaspoon black pepper
- 1 cup barbecue sauce
- 1/4 cup apple cider vinegar
- 1/4 cup brown sugar
- 1 tablespoon Worcestershire sauce
- Slider buns
- Coleslaw (optional, for topping)

Instructions:

1- Coat chicken breasts with olive oil.

2- Apply dry rub evenly and massage into the meat.

3- Cook chicken on a smoker or grill until internal temperature reaches 165°F (74°C).

4- Let the cooked chicken rest briefly.

5- Shred chicken into bite-sized pieces.

6- Simmer barbecue sauce, vinegar, sugar, and Worcestershire sauce in a saucepan.

7- Pour sauce over shredded chicken and toss to coat.

8- Place pulled chicken on buns.

9- Add coleslaw as desired.

10. Grilled Salmon with Lemon Butter

Indulge in the delicate and buttery texture of this Grilled Salmon with Lemon Butter. The combination of the grilled smokiness, tangy lemon, and rich butter elevates the natural flavors of the salmon, creating a memorable culinary experience. For a large buffet gathering, I prefer this delectable dish and savor the taste of fresh and wholesome ingredients!

Serving Size: 4 people

Marinating Time: 30 minutes (optional)

Cooking Time: 10 to 12 minutes

Ingredients:

- 4 salmon fillets (about 6 ounces each), skin-on
- 2 tablespoons olive oil
- 1 teaspoon dried dill
- 2 tablespoons fresh lemon juice
- 2 cloves garlic, minced
- 1/4 teaspoon black pepper
- 1/2 teaspoon salt
- 4 tablespoons unsalted butter, softened
- Zest of 1 lemon
- Fresh dill sprigs, for garnish (optional)

Instructions:

1- Marinate the salmon.

2- Combine softened butter and lemon zest in a bowl.

3- Remove salmon fillets from the marinade, allowing excess to drip off.

4- Grill fillets skin-side down for 5-6 minutes until crispy.

5- Flip salmon carefully and spoon lemon butter over the top.

6- Grill for another 4-6 minutes until cooked and flaky.

11. BBQ Pulled Jackfruit Sandwiches

With my love for sandwiches, I Satisfy my craving for a barbecue with these flavorful BBQ Pulled Jackfruit Sandwiches. Jackfruit, a versatile fruit that mimics the texture of pulled meat, takes center stage in this recipe. Slow-cooked in a smoky barbecue sauce and piled onto soft buns, these sandwiches are a delicious and plant-based alternative to traditional pulled pork. Get ready to sink your teeth into a hearty and satisfying meal!

Serving Size: 2 servings

Cooking Time: 40 minutes

Ingredients:

- 2 cans young green jackfruit in brine or water (not in syrup), drained and rinsed
- 1/2 onion, finely chopped
- 1 tablespoon olive oil
- 2 cloves garlic, minced
- 1/2 cup barbecue sauce (choose a vegan-friendly brand)
- 1 tablespoon tomato paste
- 1 tablespoon brown sugar or maple syrup
- 1 tablespoon apple cider vinegar
- 1 teaspoon smoked paprika
- 1/2 teaspoon cumin
- 1/2 teaspoon chili powder
- 1/4 teaspoon salt
- 1/4 teaspoon black pepper
- 4 burger buns
- Coleslaw or pickles, for topping (optional)

Instructions:

1- Rinse and dry jackfruit. Shred into pulled pork-like pieces, removing core and seeds.

2- Sauté onion and garlic in heated olive oil until soft.

3- Add shredded jackfruit to the skillet and stir with onion and garlic.

4- Combine barbecue sauce, tomato paste, brown sugar/maple syrup, vinegar, paprika, cumin, chili powder, salt, and pepper.

5- Pour sauce over jackfruit, and coat evenly.

6- Simmer on low for 30 minutes, stirring occasionally.

7- Spoon BBQ jackfruit onto toasted buns.

8- Optionally, add coleslaw or pickles.

9- Place the top bun to complete the sandwich.

12. Grilled Pineapple with Caramel Sauce

Let me Indulge you in the perfect blend of smoky and sweet flavors with this Grilled Pineapple with Caramel Sauce recipe. At times when I need fruits in my system, this is my go-to dessert. Grilling fresh pineapple slices brings out their natural sweetness and adds a delightful caramelized touch. Drizzled with a homemade caramel sauce, this dessert is a tropical treat that will satisfy your sweet tooth. Get ready to savor the taste of summer!

Serving Size: 5 servings

Grilling Time: 8 to 10 minutes

Ingredients:

- 1 ripe pineapple
- 1/4 cup brown sugar
- 1/4 cup unsalted butter, melted
- 1 teaspoon ground cinnamon
- 1/4 teaspoon salt
- Vanilla ice cream or whipped cream, for serving (optional)

For the Caramel Sauce:

- 1/2 cup granulated sugar
- 2 tablespoons water
- 3 tablespoons unsalted butter
- 1/4 cup heavy cream
- 1/2 teaspoon vanilla extract

Instructions:

1- Trim and peel the pineapple, removing eyes and tough spots.

2- Slice the pineapple into rounds or wedges.

3- Heat sugar and water in a saucepan until dissolved.

4- Let it boil until deep in amber.

5- Add butter and stir until melted and incorporated.

6- Slowly pour in heavy cream while stirring.

7- Stir in vanilla extract and set aside the caramel sauce.

8- Combine brown sugar, melted butter, cinnamon, and salt.

9- Brush pineapple slices with the mixture.

10- Grill for 4-5 minutes per side until caramelized.

11- Arrange grilled pineapple and drizzle with caramel sauce.

13. Smoked Bratwurst Sausages BBQ

The smoked bratwurst makes me enjoy this bbq piece. Fire up the grill and get ready for a smoky and flavorful feast with Smoked Bratwurst Sausages BBQ. These juicy and savory sausages are a classic favorite for barbecues and cookouts. With a hint of smokiness and a satisfying snap, they are sure to be a hit among your family and friends. Get ready to enjoy the irresistible aroma and taste of perfectly grilled bratwurst sausages!

Serving Size: 8 servings

Cooking Time: 15 to 20 minutes

Ingredients:

- 8 bratwurst sausages
- 1 tablespoon olive oil
- 1 onion, thinly sliced
- 2 cloves garlic, minced
- 1/2 teaspoon dried thyme
- 1/2 teaspoon dried rosemary
- 1/2 teaspoon paprika
- 1/2 teaspoon salt
- 1/4 teaspoon black pepper
- Mustard and sauerkraut

Instructions:

1- Heat olive oil in a skillet over medium heat.

2- Sauté onions and garlic until golden brown.

3- Set aside.

4- Mix dried thyme, dried rosemary, paprika, salt, and black pepper in a bowl to create a seasoning blend.

5- Pat dry the bratwurst sausages.

6- Coat the sausages with the seasoning blend.

7- Grill the sausages, turning occasionally, until browned and cooked through (15-20 minutes).

14. BBQ Pork Belly Burnt Ends

No doubt, I Enjoy this delectable BBQ Pork Belly Burnt Ends, with their smoky, sweet, and savory flavors. These irresistible bites are sure to be the highlight of any barbecue gathering, impressing your family and friends with their tender texture and mouthwatering taste.

Serving Size: 12 people

Cooking Time: 4 to 5 hours

Ingredients:

- 2 pounds pork belly, skin removed
- 2 tablespoons barbecue rub (store-bought or homemade)
- 1/4 cup brown sugar
- 1/4 cup honey
- 1/4 cup barbecue sauce (choose your favorite)
- 2 tablespoons butter, melted
- 1 tablespoon apple cider vinegar
- 1 teaspoon Worcestershire sauce
- Salt and black pepper to taste
- Smoked wood chips (such as hickory or apple), soaked in water for at least 30 minutes

Instructions:

1- Trim excess fat from the pork belly and cut into cubes.

2- Combine barbecue rub, brown sugar, salt, and black pepper.

3- Sprinkle the mixture over the pork cubes.

4- Smoke for 2-3 hours until a bark forms.

5- Combine honey, barbecue sauce, melted butter, vinegar, and Worcestershire sauce to create a glaze.

6- Pour glaze over the cubes.

7- Cook for 1.5-2 hours until tender and the glaze thickens.

8- Let the burnt ends cool.

15. Grilled Portobello Mushroom Burgers

I love to Savor the deliciousness of these Grilled Portobello Mushroom Burgers, perfect for vegetarians and vegans. With their rich flavors and satisfying texture, these burgers provide a wholesome and tasty alternative to traditional meat-based options. Gather your friends and family, fire up the grill, and enjoy a fantastic plant-based burger experience!

Serving Size: 4 servings

Marinating Time: 30 minutes

Cooking Time: 10 to 12 minutes

Ingredients:

- 4 large portobello mushroom caps
- 1/4 cup balsamic vinegar
- 2 tablespoons olive oil
- 2 tablespoons soy sauce or tamari (for a gluten-free option)
- 2 cloves garlic, minced
- 1 teaspoon dried thyme
- 1 teaspoon dried rosemary
- Salt and black pepper to taste
- Burger buns
- Toppings of your choice (lettuce, tomato, onion, avocado, etc.)

Instructions:

1- Whisk balsamic vinegar, olive oil, salt, soy sauce, dried thyme, minced garlic, dried rosemary, and black pepper in a dish.

2- Marinate portobello mushroom caps in the mixture for at least 30 minutes.

3- Lightly oil grill grates.

4- Grill marinated mushroom caps, brushing with reserved marinade.

5- Grill for 5 to 6 minutes per side until tender with grill marks.

6- Brush caps with marinade while grilling.

7- Transfer grilled mushroom caps to a plate.

8- Place each cap on a bun.

9- Add desired toppings.

10- Serve with fries or salad for a complete meal.

16. BBQ Bacon-Wrapped Jalapeno Poppers

I spice up my barbecue with these irresistible BBQ Bacon-Wrapped Jalapeno Poppers. I love how this delicious appetizer combines the heat of jalapeno peppers, the creaminess of cheese filling, and the smoky flavor of crispy bacon. Grilled to perfection and slathered with barbecue sauce, these poppers are the perfect balance of spicy, cheesy, and savory. They are guaranteed to be a hit at your next gathering or game-day party!

Serving Size: 6 servings

Cooking Time: 15 to 20 minutes

Ingredients:

- 12 jalapeno peppers
- 6 slices of bacon, cut in half
- 4 ounces cream cheese, softened
- 1/2 cup shredded cheddar cheese
- 1/2 teaspoon garlic powder
- 1/2 teaspoon onion powder
- 1/4 teaspoon paprika
- 1/4 teaspoon cayenne pepper (optional, for extra heat)
- Barbecue sauce, for brushing

Instructions:

1- Preheat the grill to medium heat (350°F to 375°F, or 175°C to 190°C).

2- Slice jalapeno peppers in half lengthwise.

3- Remove seeds and membranes from jalapeno halves.

4- Rinse jalapeno halves under cold water.

5- In a bowl, mix softened cream cheese, shredded cheddar cheese, garlic powder, onion powder, paprika, and cayenne pepper (optional).

6- Fill jalapeno halves with cheese mixture.

7- Wrap each stuffed jalapeno with a bacon slice, securing it with a toothpick.

8- Place poppers on the grill and cook for 15 to 20 minutes until bacon is crispy and jalapenos are tender.

9- Brush poppers with barbecue sauce in the last 5 minutes of cooking.

10- Allow the sauce to caramelize slightly before serving.

17. Teriyaki Glazed Grilled Steak

Along with family and friends, I Enjoy the mouthwatering flavors of tender and juicy Teriyaki Glazed Grilled Steak. This recipe combines the rich umami taste of teriyaki sauce with perfectly grilled steak, resulting in a delightful fusion of sweet and savory flavors. Whether you're hosting a barbecue or looking to elevate your weeknight dinner, this recipe is sure to impress and satisfy your cravings for a delicious grilled steak.

Serving Size: 2 servings

Marinating Time: 30 minutes to 2 hours

Cooking Time: 10 to 15 minutes

Ingredients:

- 2 pounds of steak (such as ribeye, sirloin, or flank steak)
- 1/2 cup teriyaki sauce (store-bought or homemade)
- 2 tablespoons soy sauce
- 2 tablespoons honey
- 2 cloves garlic, minced
- 1 tablespoon ginger, grated
- 1 tablespoon sesame oil
- 1 tablespoon vegetable oil
- Salt and black pepper, to taste
- Optional garnish: sesame seeds, green onions

Instructions:

1- Marinate the steak with the marinade. Remove excess marinade from the steak.

2- Season with salt and black pepper.

3- Grill the steak for 4 to 6 minutes per side.

4- Brush with teriyaki sauce in the last 2 minutes for a glaze.

5- Let the steak rest to redistribute juices.

6- Tent with foil while resting.

7- Slice the steak thinly against the grain.

18. Grilled Watermelon and Feta Salad

Elevate your summer barbecue with a refreshing and vibrant Grilled Watermelon and Feta Salad. This unique salad combines the sweetness of grilled watermelon with the creamy saltiness of feta cheese, balanced with a tangy dressing and fresh herbs. With a delightful combination of flavors and textures, I impress my guests and add a burst of color to our BBQ spread. Get ready to enjoy a light and refreshing salad that celebrates the best of summer!

Serving Size: 4 People

Grilling Time: 4 to 6 minutes

Ingredients:

- 4 to 5 thick slices of watermelon, cut into wedges or triangles
- 4 ounces feta cheese, crumbled
- 1/4 cup fresh mint leaves, torn or chopped
- 1/4 cup fresh basil leaves, torn or chopped
- 2 tablespoons extra-virgin olive oil
- 1 tablespoon balsamic glaze
- Salt and black pepper, to taste

Instructions:

1- Grill watermelon wedges until slightly softened with grill marks.

2- Let the grilled watermelon cool, then cut it into bite-sized pieces.

3- Place watermelon pieces in a serving bowl or platter.

4- Sprinkle crumbled feta cheese, torn/chopped mint leaves, and basil leaves.

5- Drizzle olive oil and balsamic glaze over the salad.

6- Season with salt and black pepper.

7- Serve immediately as a refreshing side dish or appetizer.

19. Smoked Turkey Legs

Get ready to savor the smoky goodness and tender juiciness of these mouthwatering Smoked Turkey Legs. Whether at a summer cookout or a festive gathering, I enjoy these turkey legs as they are sure to be a hit. Indulge in the irresistible flavors and the nostalgia of fair food with this delectable barbecue treat!

Serving Size: 4 people

Cooking Time: 3 to 4 hours

Ingredients:

- 4 turkey legs
- 1/4 cup kosher salt (for brine, optional)
- 1/4 cup brown sugar (for brine, optional)
- 1 tablespoon paprika
- 1 tablespoon garlic powder
- 1 tablespoon onion powder
- 1 tablespoon black pepper
- 1 teaspoon dried thyme
- 1 teaspoon dried rosemary
- 1 teaspoon cayenne pepper (adjust to taste)
- Olive oil, for brushing
- Wood chips or chunks (such as hickory or apple), soaked in water for at least 30 minutes

Instructions:

1- Brine the Turkey Legs.

2- In a small bowl, combine the paprika, garlic powder, onion powder, black pepper, dried thyme, dried rosemary, and cayenne pepper.

3- Remove the turkey legs from the brine and pat them dry with paper towels.

4- Sprinkle the spice mixture evenly over the turkey legs, pressing it onto the surface to adhere.

5- Smoke the turkey legs for 3 to 4 hours

6- Remove the turkey legs from the smoker or grill and let them rest for 10 minutes to allow the juices to redistribute.

20. Honey Mustard BBQ Chicken Drumsticks

I Delight my taste buds with the irresistible combination of sweet and tangy flavors in these Honey Mustard BBQ Chicken Drumsticks. The succulent chicken drumsticks are coated in a sticky and flavorful honey mustard sauce, resulting in a finger-licking barbecue experience. Whether you're grilling outdoors or using the oven, these chicken drumsticks are perfect for a summer cookout or a weeknight dinner. Get ready to savor the juicy and flavorful goodness!

Serving Size: 8 Servings

Marinating Time: 30 minutes to 2 hours

Cooking Time: 35 to 45 minutes

Ingredients:

- 8 chicken drumsticks
- 1/3 cup honey
- 1/4 cup Dijon mustard
- 2 tablespoons barbecue sauce
- 2 tablespoons soy sauce
- 1 tablespoon olive oil
- 2 cloves garlic, minced
- 1 teaspoon paprika
- 1/2 teaspoon salt
- 1/4 teaspoon black pepper
- Optional garnish: chopped fresh parsley or green onions

Instructions:

1- Make the Honey Mustard BBQ Sauce.

2- Marinate the chicken drumsticks.

3- Grill for 35 to 45 minutes or bake for the same duration.

4- Baste with additional sauce during the last 10 minutes.

5- Remove from the grill or oven.

6- Garnish with fresh parsley or green onions (optional).

21. Grilled Halloumi Skewers

This recipe is a discovery! I Elevate my barbecue with these delicious Grilled Halloumi Skewers. Halloumi, a firm, salty cheese, becomes beautifully charred and slightly melted when grilled, resulting in a delightful combination of flavors and textures. These skewers are perfect for vegetarian or cheese-loving guests at your barbecue party. Get ready to enjoy a unique and tasty grilled appetizer that will impress your friends and family!

Serving Size: 2 Servings

Marinating Time: 30 minutes

Cooking Time: 6 to 8 minutes

Ingredients:

- 8 ounces of halloumi cheese
- 1 red bell pepper
- 1 yellow bell pepper
- 1 zucchini
- 1 red onion
- 2 tablespoons olive oil
- 1 tablespoon lemon juice
- 1 teaspoon dried oregano
- 1/2 teaspoon garlic powder
- Salt and black pepper, to taste
- Optional garnish: Fresh parsley or mint leaves

Instructions:

1- Prepare Halloumi and vegetables.

2- Whisk together olive oil, lemon juice, oregano, garlic powder, salt, and black pepper.

3- Marinate Halloumi and vegetables.

4- Coat halloumi and vegetables with marinade and refrigerate for 30 minutes.

5- Skewer marinated halloumi and vegetables, leaving space between each piece.

6- Place skewers on a preheated grill.

7- Grill until halloumi is charred and slightly softened, and vegetables are tender-crisp.

8- Remove from the grill and let it cool briefly.

22. BBQ Pulled Lamb Tacos

Elevate your taco game with these flavorful BBQ Pulled Lamb Tacos. I crave the Tender and succulent pulled lamb, slow-cooked in a rich and smoky barbecue sauce. Piled into warm tortillas and topped with fresh and vibrant toppings, these tacos are a delicious fusion of barbecue and Mexican cuisine. Get ready to indulge in a mouthwatering taco experience that will satisfy your cravings!

Serving Size: 4 to 6 servings

Cooking Time: 4 to 6 hours

Ingredients:

For the BBQ Pulled Lamb:

- 2 pounds boneless lamb shoulder or leg
- 1 cup barbecue sauce
- 1 teaspoon smoked paprika
- 1/4 teaspoon black pepper
- 1/4 cup apple cider vinegar
- 2 tablespoons brown sugar
- 2 cloves garlic, minced
- 1/2 teaspoon cumin
- 1/2 teaspoon salt

For the Tacos:

- 12 small flour or corn tortillas
- 1 cup diced tomatoes
- 1/2 cup diced red onion
- 1 cup shredded lettuce
- 1/4 cup chopped fresh cilantro
- Lime wedges, for serving

Instructions:

1- Trim excess fat from the lamb and cut it into large chunks.

2- Create barbecue sauce and pour it over the lamb.

3- Cook in a slow cooker or pot on low heat for 6-8 hours or high heat for 4-6 hours until tender.

4- Shred the cooked lamb using two forks.

5- Warm tortillas and place BBQ-pulled lamb on each.

6- Top with lettuce, tomatoes, red onion, and cilantro.

7- Squeeze lime juice over the tacos.

8- Arrange on a platter and serve.

23. Grilled Caesar Salad

Without extra stress, I Give my classic Caesar salad a smoky twist with this Grilled Caesar Salad recipe. Crisp romaine lettuce is lightly grilled to add a hint of charred flavor, while the creamy Caesar dressing and crunchy croutons bring all the traditional elements together. This salad is a perfect side dish for your barbecue or a refreshing main course on its own. Get ready to enjoy a unique and delicious take on a timeless salad favorite!

Serving Size: 4 Servings

Cooking Time: 10 minutes

Ingredients:

- 2 large heads of romaine lettuce
- Olive oil, for brushing
- Salt and black pepper, to taste
- 1/2 cup mayonnaise
- 2 tablespoons freshly squeezed lemon juice
- 2 tablespoons grated Parmesan cheese
- 2 cloves garlic, minced
- 1 teaspoon Dijon mustard
- 1 anchovy fillet, minced (optional)
- Salt and black pepper, to taste
- 2 cups bread cubes (such as French bread or ciabatta)
- 2 tablespoons olive oil
- 1/2 teaspoon garlic powder
- Salt and black pepper, to taste
- Shaved Parmesan cheese
- Lemon wedges

Instructions:

1- Slice the romaine lettuce heads lengthwise, keeping the core intact.

2- Brush with olive oil, sprinkle salt and pepper.

3- Grill cut side down for 2-3 minutes until charred.

4- Flip and grill for another 2-3 minutes.

5- Transfer grilled lettuce to a platter.

Caesar Dressing:

1- Whisk mayo, lemon juice, Parmesan, garlic, Dijon mustard, and anchovy.

2- Season with salt and pepper.

Croutons:

1- Toss bread cubes with oil, garlic powder, salt, and pepper.

2- Bake for 10 minutes until crispy.

To Serve:

1- Drizzle Caesar dressing over lettuce.

2- Sprinkle with croutons.

3- Garnish with shaved Parmesan and serve with lemon wedges. Enjoy!

24. Korean BBQ Beef Bulgogi

This mouthwatering Korean BBQ Beef Bulgogi recipe always transports my taste buds to Korea. Thinly sliced beef marinated in a flavorful blend of soy sauce, sesame oil, garlic, and other aromatics, grilled to perfection and served with a side of rice and assorted toppings. I savor this popular Korean dish for its tender and savory flavors, making it a hit at any barbecue or gathering. Get ready to enjoy a delicious and satisfying meal that will leave you craving more!

Marinating Time: 1 to 2 hours

Cooking Time: 10 minutes

Serving: 4 servings

Ingredients:

- 5 pounds thinly sliced beef (such as ribeye or sirloin)
- 1/4 cup soy sauce
- 2 tablespoons sesame oil
- 2 cloves garlic, minced
- 1 tablespoon grated ginger
- 2 tablespoons brown sugar
- 1 tablespoon rice vinegar
- 1 tablespoon mirin (sweet rice wine, optional)
- 1 tablespoon sesame seeds
- 2 green onions, thinly sliced
- Freshly ground black pepper, to taste
- Vegetable oil, for grilling
- Cooked rice, for serving
- Assorted toppings (such as sliced cucumbers, carrots, lettuce, and kimchi)

Instructions:

1- Combine soy sauce, brown sugar, sesame oil, minced garlic, grated ginger, rice vinegar, mirin (optional), sesame seeds, sliced green onions, and black pepper to create the marinade.

2- Coat thinly sliced beef with the marinade and refrigerate for 1 to 2 hours or overnight.

3- Preheat and lightly oil the grill or grill pan.

4- Grill the beef slices for 2 to 3 minutes per side.

5- Let the grilled beef rest before serving.

25. Smoked Sausage and Potato Foil Packets BBQ

For large gatherings, I Add some smoky goodness to my barbecue with this delicious Smoked Sausage and Potato Foil Packets. This easy and flavorful recipe combines smoky sausage, tender potatoes, and a medley of vegetables, all cooked together in a convenient foil packet. The ingredients are seasoned with herbs and spices, and the foil packet locks in the flavors while ensuring a moist and delicious result. These foil packets are perfect for outdoor gatherings and make for a satisfying and fuss-free meal. Get ready to enjoy a hearty and flavorful dish straight from the grill!

Cooking Time: 25 minutes

Serving: 4 servings

Ingredients:

- 1 pound smoked sausage, sliced into rounds
- 4 medium potatoes, diced into 1-inch cubes
- 1 red bell pepper, sliced
- 1 green bell pepper, sliced
- 1 onion, thinly sliced
- 2 cloves garlic, minced
- 1/2 teaspoon onion powder
- 2 tablespoons olive oil
- 1 teaspoon smoked paprika
- 1 teaspoon dried thyme
- 1/2 teaspoon garlic powder
- Salt and black pepper, to taste
- Fresh parsley, chopped (for garnish)

Instructions:

1- Distribute sausage, potatoes, bell peppers, and onion evenly on foil sheets.

2- Mix seasoning.

3- Drizzle seasoning over the ingredients in each foil packet.

4- Toss ingredients to coat evenly.

5- Seal foil packets tightly.

6- Ensure packets are closed to trap steam and flavors.

7- Grill packets with the lid closed.

8- Cook for 20-25 minutes until potatoes are tender and sausage is cooked.

9- Rotate packets for even cooking.

10- Transfer contents to plates or bowls.

26. BBQ Pulled Chicken Pizza

This homemade BBQ pizza features a crispy crust topped with tender pulled chicken coated in tangy BBQ sauce. Along with a medley of colorful vegetables and melty cheese, I always crave more. It's the perfect fusion of barbecue and pizza flavors, making it a crowd-pleasing dish for any occasion. Get ready to delight your taste buds with this mouthwatering pizza creation!

Cooking Time: 15-20 minutes

Serving: 4-6 servings

Ingredients:

- 1 pizza dough (store-bought or homemade)
- 1 cup cooked and shredded chicken breast
- 1/2 yellow bell pepper, thinly sliced
- Olive oil, for brushing
- 1/4 cup chopped fresh cilantro
- 1/2 cup corn kernels
- 1/2 red bell pepper, thinly sliced
- 1/2 red onion, thinly sliced
- 1 cup shredded mozzarella cheese
- 1/2 cup barbecue sauce

Instructions:

1- Combine the shredded chicken with BBQ sauce.

2- Roll out pizza dough and transfer it to a baking surface.

3- Brush dough with olive oil. Spread BBQ sauce on the dough.

4- Add cheese, chicken, and vegetables. Bake for 15-20 minutes. Let it cool slightly. Sprinkle with cilantro.

5- Slice and serve hot.

27. Grilled Zucchini Rolls with Goat Cheese

Whenever I am craving zucchini rolls, this is always my resort. These Grilled Zucchini Rolls with Goat Cheese are a light and refreshing appetizer that combines the natural sweetness of grilled zucchini with the creamy tanginess of goat cheese. The fresh herbs and lemon zest add a bright and zesty touch. Whether you're hosting a party or simply looking for a flavorful snack, these zucchini rolls are sure to impress your guests and leave them wanting more.

Cooking Time: 10 minutes

Serving: 4-6 servings

Ingredients:

- 2 medium zucchinis
- 4 ounces of goat cheese
- 1 tablespoon fresh basil, chopped
- 1 tablespoon fresh mint, chopped
- 1 tablespoon fresh parsley, chopped
- 1 tablespoon lemon zest
- 1 tablespoon lemon juice
- Salt and black pepper, to taste
- Olive oil, for grilling

Instructions:

To prepare zucchini:

1- Trim and slice zucchinis lengthwise into thin strips.

2- Brush with olive oil, season with salt and pepper.

3- Grill for 2-3 minutes per side.

4- Let the grilled zucchini cool.

To prepare goat cheese filling:

1- Combine goat cheese, basil, mint, parsley, lemon zest, and juice.

2- Season with salt and pepper and mix well.

To assemble:

1- Lay a grilled zucchini strip flat.

2- Spread goat cheese filling evenly.

3- Roll tightly to create a compact roll.

4- Repeat with the remaining zucchini and filling.

5- Arrange on a platter.

6- Garnish with herbs or lemon zest.

7- Serve at room temperature. Enjoy!

28. Smoked BBQ Meatballs

Get ready for a flavor explosion with these Smoked BBQ Meatballs! I love how these meatballs are marinated. These tender and juicy meatballs are infused with smoky goodness from the barbecue smoker, then glazed with a tangy and sweet barbecue sauce. Whether you serve them as an appetizer or as a main dish, these smoked meatballs will be a hit at your next gathering or family meal. Fire up your smoker and prepare for a mouthwatering meatball experience!

Grilling Time: 2-3 hours

Serving: 4-6 servings

Ingredients:

For the Meatballs:

- 1 ½ pounds of ground beef
- ½ pound ground pork
- 1 small onion, finely chopped
- 2 garlic cloves, minced
- 1 egg, lightly beaten
- ½ cup breadcrumbs
- 2 tablespoons milk
- 1 teaspoon salt
- ½ teaspoon black pepper
- ½ teaspoon smoked paprika
- ½ teaspoon dried oregano
- ½ teaspoon dried thyme

For the BBQ Sauce:

- 1 cup ketchup
- ¼ cup brown sugar
- ½ teaspoon onion powder
- 2 tablespoons apple cider vinegar
- 1 tablespoon Worcestershire sauce
- 1 tablespoon Dijon mustard
- 1 teaspoon smoked paprika
- ½ teaspoon garlic powder
- Salt and black pepper, to taste

Instructions:

1- Combine ground beef, ground pork, onion, garlic, egg, breadcrumbs, milk, and seasonings. Shape into meatballs and smoke for 2-3 hours at 160°F.

2- Make BBQ sauce by simmering ingredients.

3- Brush meatballs with sauce and smoke for 15-20 minutes more.

4- Serve with garnish and extra sauce.

29. Grilled Peaches with Vanilla Ice Cream

Looking for a twist in your summer treat? I recommend this recipe. Grilled Peaches with Vanilla Ice Cream is a summer treat that combines the natural sweetness of peaches with the smoky flavors from the grill. The caramelized edges of the peaches paired with the cool and creamy vanilla ice cream create a harmonious and satisfying dessert. It's a simple yet impressive way to end a summer meal on a sweet note.

Grilling Time: 10 minutes

Serving: 4 servings

Ingredients:

- 4 ripe peaches
- 2 tablespoons melted butter
- 2 tablespoons brown sugar
- 1 teaspoon ground cinnamon
- Vanilla ice cream, for serving
- Honey or caramel sauce, for drizzling
- Fresh mint leaves, for garnish

Instructions:

1- Cut the peaches in half and remove the pits.

2- Brush with melted butter.

3- Grill cut-side down until marked and softened.

4- Flip and grill for 2 more minutes.

5- Mix brown sugar and cinnamon. Sprinkle over grilled peaches.

6- Grill cut-side up.

7- Cook with a closed lid until sugar caramelizes.

8- Serve warm with vanilla ice cream.

30. BBQ Pulled Beef Sliders

BBQ Pulled Beef Sliders are the ultimate crowd-pleaser, combining rich and tender beef with the bold flavors of barbecue sauce. I enjoy this due to the beef sliders. They are perfect for serving at parties, potlucks, or even as a simple and delicious weeknight meal. Get ready to savor the irresistible combination of tender beef, tangy sauce, and soft buns in every bite.

Cooking Time: 6-8 hours (slow cooker) or 4-5 hours (grill)

Serving: 8-10 servings

Ingredients:

- 2 pounds beef chuck roast
- 1 onion, thinly sliced
- 3 cloves garlic, minced
- 1 cup beef broth
- 1 cup barbecue sauce
- 2 tablespoons brown sugar
- 2 tablespoons apple cider vinegar
- 1 tablespoon Worcestershire sauce
- 1 teaspoon smoked paprika
- 1 teaspoon garlic powder
- 1 teaspoon onion powder
- Salt and black pepper, to taste
- Slider buns, for serving
- Coleslaw, sliced pickles, or any desired toppings

Instructions:

1- Prepare the beef by seasoning and searing it.

2- Place it in a foil pan with onions and garlic.

3- Pour a mixture of broth, barbecue sauce, sugar, vinegar, and Worcestershire sauce over the beef.

4- Cook on low heat for 4-5 hours until tender.

5- Shred the beef and coat it in BBQ sauce.

6- Assemble the sliders by placing the pulled beef on buns and adding toppings.

7- Serve immediately.

Conclusion

On a final note, Summer BBQ Fiesta: 30 Barbecue Recipes for Summer Partaay is your ultimate guide to creating unforgettable culinary experiences at your summer parties. These recipes not only satisfy your taste buds but also ignite a sense of togetherness and celebration. From juicy grilled meats to delectable sides and tantalizing sauces.

This cookbook transcends borders and unites cultures through the universal language of food. With each recipe, you'll embark on a flavorful adventure, infusing your own creativity and personal touch. So, gather your loved ones, fire up the grill, and let Summer BBQ Fiesta be your go-to companion for memorable summer parties filled with laughter, good food, and cherished moments.

Let the BBQ fiesta begin!

Appendices

Thank you ♥

Hey, guys! I just wanted to say thanks for supporting me by purchasing one of my e-books. I have to say—when I first started writing cookbooks, I didn't have many expectations for myself because it was never a part of "the plan." It was more of a hobby, something I did for me and decided to put out there if someone might click on my book and buy it because they liked my food. Well, let me just say it's been a while since those days, and it's been a wild journey!

Now, cookbook writing is a huge part of my life, and I'm doing things I love! So, THANK YOU for trusting me with your weekly meal preps, weekend BBQs, 10-minute dinners, and all of your special occasions. If it weren't for you, I wouldn't be able to concentrate on producing all sorts of delicious recipes, which is why I've decided to reach out and ask for your help. What kind of recipes would you like to see more of? Are you interested in special diets, foods made with kitchen appliances, or just easy recipes on a time-crunch? Your input will help me create books you want to read with recipes you'll actually make! Make sure to let me know, and your suggestions could trigger an idea for my next book…

Take care!

Owen

Printed in Great Britain
by Amazon

31167592R00051